Andrea Gess ✝♡

andrea.gess@gmail.com

304-685-3076

Rom. 15:13

Prov. 3:5-6

Jer. 29:11

eight
steps to a
brand new
life

eight
steps to a
brand new
life

david baird

PUBLISHING

ISBN: 978-0-9795489-8-7

Published by Making Life Better Publishing
14411 Presidents Landing Way
Gainesville, VA 20155
www.mlbpublishing.com

Printed in Colombia

Your 8-Day Coach:

_____

Contact Your Coach

Coach's Phone:

_____

Coach's E-mail:

_____

Coach's Facebook:

_____

8daycoaching.com

Table of Contents

the new birth
john 3:5-8

"Jesus answered, 'I tell you the truth, no one can enter the kingdom of God unless he is born of water and the Spirit. Flesh gives birth to flesh, but the Spirit gives birth to spirit. You should not be surprised at my saying, "You must be born again." The wind blows wherever it pleases. You hear its sound, but you cannot tell where it comes from or where it is going. So it is with everyone born of the Spirit."

Preface
You've Been Born Again

Congratulations. You've been born again! You have prayed a prayer asking God to save you! When you prayed this prayer, something incredible happened. God gave you a new life. A new birth occurred inside of you as God came to live in your spirit! It's an incredible miracle, even though we can't fully explain it. After all, can human birth be fully explained? No, despite science, it's still a wonder and an awe to witness a natural birth. The same with our supernatural birth.

What we do know is this. We have been given a spiritual birth and a potential to have a brand new life.

Now the journey toward living out this new life begins and this what the "eight steps" are all about. We've extracted eight steps taken by the "prodigal son" in his journey back home and these same steps are yours to take as you begin your "journey home." It's a journey back to your "predestination" and ahead to the new realities of living with your God-given purpose at the center of your being.

I encourage you to read, watch and talk each day.

Read a chapter from this book everyday that corresponds to each step.

Watch the corresponding video clip for each day at www.8daycoaching.com.

Finally, talk to your coach each day. His number and email are written in the front of the book. If it's missing, go to the 8daycoaching.com and request a coach be assigned to you.

Coaching is God's way for all. When Paul (who was then named Saul) got converted in Bible days, he experienced a supernatural conversion on the "road" to Damascus (Acts 9:1-9). But immediately after that great conversion, God assigned a coach to him (Acts 9:10-19). His name was Annanias and he helped Saul get started on the new road to his brand new life. This is our prayer for you. We're cheering you on and know you've made the best decision of your life.

Welcome to your brand new life!

our story
luke 15:11-24

the parable of the lost son

Jesus continued: "There was a man who had two sons. The younger one said to his father, 'Father, give me my share of the estate.' So he divided his property between them.

Not long after that, the younger son got together all he had, set off for a distant country and there squandered his wealth in wild living. After he had spent everything, there was a severe famine in that whole country, and he began to be in need. So he went and hired himself out to a citizen of that country, who sent him to his fields to feed pigs. He longed to fill his stomach with the pods that the pigs were eating, but no one gave him anything.

When he came to his senses, he said, 'How many of my father's hired men have food to spare, and here I am starving to death! I will

set out and go back to my father and say to him:
Father, I have sinned against heaven and against
you. I am no longer worthy to be called your son;
make me like one of your hired men.' So he got
up and went to his father.

But while he was still a long way off, his
father saw him and was filled with compassion
for him; he ran to his son, threw his arms around
him and kissed him.

The son said to him, 'Father, I have sinned
against heaven and against you. I am no longer
worthy to be called your son.'

But the father said to his servants, 'Quick!
Bring the best robe and put it on him. Put a ring
on his finger and sandals on his feet. Bring the
fattened calf and kill it. Let's have a feast and
celebrate. For this son of mine was dead and is
alive again; he was lost and is found.' So they
began to celebrate."

step one
wake up

realize your need for God
"He came to his senses."
(Luke 15:17)

eight
steps to a
brand new
life

The story of the Prodigal son is considered one of the greatest stories ever told. It's a picture of all of us who have lost our way. It's a picture of our heavenly Father wooing us back home. It's a story of what is lost being found. It's a story that contrasts old religion to the joy of the Kingdom of God.

The younger son asks for his inheritance and leaves home. He chooses a way that seems right to him at the time, yet he ends up in a life of destruction. The consequences of this destructive behavior is symbolized by the pig pen. It's the classic riches to rags story of wasted living. But it's also a story of the way back from rags to riches.

It's a story with steps taken by the lost son as he seeks to find his way home.

It's our model for finding our way back home.

The first step is to wake up. The lost son came to his senses in the pig pen. His depraved condition woke him him up. A starving man is a desperate man. God used the depravity of the pig pen to bring the lost son to his senses. And God uses our depravity and the circumstances it has produced to wake us up.

The only way to come to God is by taking off masks created by deceitful thinking. The real you has to meet the real God, for God is a person.

Your heart easily goes askew. That's okay. You have to begin with what is real. Jesus didn't come for the righteous. He came for sinners. All of us qualify. The very things we try to get rid of—our weariness, our distractedness, our messiness—are what get us in the front door! That's how the gospel works. That's how prayer works.

In bringing your real self to Jesus, you give him the opportunity to work on the real you, and you will change. The kingdom comes when Jesus becomes king of your life. But it has to be your life. You can't create a kingdom that doesn't exist, where you try to be better than you really are. Jesus calls that hypocrisy—putting on a mask to cover the real you.

Instead of being paralyzed by who you are, begin with who you are. That's how the gospel works. God begins with you. Realize your need for God. Don't run from your problems. Allow them to be the agency through which you hear the voice of God.

Today you responded to God. More than

likely, that response was generated by the reality of your situation. That's okay. God has used your "pig pen" to alert your senses to the need for a change. God uses our sin and its consequences to deliver a reality check that can catapult us into a new direction. The day of the "same old, same old" is over. You have taken the first step to a whole new life. When you look back, you will see how your "mess" was used by God to create the "message" of your new life.

Yet right now you still feel vulnerable and exposed. That's okay. It's a good place to be. You're not asleep any longer. You're out of denial. That's the good news. You see your need. God has come to you and awakened you. What a great place to be.

Thought to Ponder

What circumstances or realities in
your life triggered you to make a
decision to respond to God today?

Can you now see how God has used
your mess to speak to you?

step two
get up

make a decision to change
"So he got up." (Luke 15:20)

eight
steps to a
brand new
life

The prodigal is in the pig pen. There he decides to get up. He makes the decision to change. This is what you have done when you responded to God and asked God to give you a new life.

Too often we wait for our circumstances to change. We say, "God, if you'll change my circumstances, I will give you my life." But in our story, the lost son makes this decision to change while mired down in the mud of the pen. His present reality encountered a remembrance of the way it was back home. "How many of my father's hired men have food to spare, and here I am starving to death!"

There is a better place than the place produced by sin. Life doesn't have to be the way it's always been. It doesn't have to be this hard. And it is the remembrance of a better life that provokes us to reach for something better.

You must make this decision to change today and every day as you begin your journey home. There is something inside of you that says life doesn't have to be this way. I can change. There is a better way.

The Bible calls this "eternity." He has set eternity in our hearts. (Ecclesiastes 3:11)

There is the call to change put in our

hearts by God. It's the call of heaven to all of us who live on the earth. It's what happens when we are born again. We pass from death to life (John 5:24) and something about what drives us changes. The desire to change is instilled in us by God. We no longer can be content to live mediocre, unfulfilled lives. There is something more and we've decided to get up and go after it. We are made for more and we will not be content to continue to live in a pig pen.

I encourage you to not be discouraged with your present situation. God has put change in your heart and now you are deciding to act on it. The fact that you responded to God started the process of getting up from where you are and going for something greater. The fact that you are reading about this step on the day after is further evidence you want to change.

Don't allow frustration to set in and "dis" your courage. You are not too far gone. You are not destined to stay the way you are. You are not destined to stay imprisoned to your present reality. You can change! This is your declaration, but it's also your prayer. "God, you can change; me, that is." This is my prayer.

Your willpower is not the answer. Your

will and your power have failed you, probably
over and over again. Now it's time for God's will
and God's power to be trusted. God has a will
for your life, a will that He will execute if you will
trust Him. God also has the power to produce
this change in you, but you must surrender your
will to His will and your self-sufficiency to His
power.

There is a better place to live, and, as far
as it may seem from here, it's still a much better
place to be than where you are now. Know today
that God has destined you for that better place.
Make the decision to get up and go there.

Thought to Ponder

What are some thoughts, actions and habits that I need to change that constantly bring me down?

step three
go home

get back on track
"He went to his father."
(Luke 15:20)

eight
steps to a
brand new
life

The first step to a brand new life is realizing you are headed in the wrong direction. The second step is to turn around and head in a new direction. This is the commitment to change. But where does change lead you? Back home. The prodigal came to his senses, got up, and headed home. He went to his Father.

It's called getting back on track. When we receive Christ, we get back on track. We head home.

Home is where we started out and it's where we're intended to live. It represents the original design for our lives. It represents our intended place in the Father's plan. It's where our story begins. Our story begins in the Father's house, not in the pig pen. The pig pen represents the place we got off track. The act of accepting Christ into our life signifies our desire to get back on track.

Your story begins with your creation. God made you in His image. You were made to be somebody. You were created with a God-given personality, potential, and purpose.

Enter sin. This is how we got off track. Sin is when we choose to rely on our own ways and leave God out of the decision-making moments of our lives. It causes us to "miss the mark" that is on our life from our original, upright creation. In other words, our life begins with a unique, God-given destiny. This is "home." The pig pen represents the result of our sinfulness.

And we all have sinned. There are no big sins and no little sins. Sin is sin when it comes to God. It causes us to miss the mark. All sin leads us into this pig pen. That is why Jesus came to the earth. He died to deal with our sin and offer a restored relationship back to God. He becomes "the Way." This way leads us back home, to our original destiny. Everything lost by sin-- our potential, our purpose in life, our dynamic person--is restored in Jesus Christ. You're already back on track because you have received the forgiveness of sins through the work of Christ. Now you walk out this step of getting back on track.

The power of those sinful forces in your life that got you off track is broken by the power of the cross! You're back on track and headed home. *It's the best place on earth!*

Thought to Ponder

How did I get off track?

What lost ground do I need to
reclaim over my life?

step four
get hugged

see God in a new light
"His father saw him and was filled
with compassion for him; he ran to
his son, threw his arms around him
and kissed him." (Luke 15:20)

eight
steps to a
brand new
life

Now that you're back on track and headed home, you need to prepare for a whole new way of relating to the Father. We serve one God, who in the Bible is revealed as Father, Son, and Spirit. Christians call this the Trinity. God is first Father and we can't know God properly if we don't have a healthy view of Him as our loving Father.

This is one of the most interesting things about our story. The Prodigal heads home and the Father runs to welcome him. He runs, warmly embraces, and kisses his lost son. What a picture of what has happened to you. The Father ran to you, threw His arms around you and fell on you. He had compassion on you and has embraced you with open arms.

What a different image many have of God! We may see God without any compassion. We may see Him waiting on us rather than running to us. Some see Him harsh and cold without a warm embrace, but He's just the opposite. He is a God filled with love and compassion. He is not withholding, but open to receive us.

We need to see the act of receiving God in our hearts as His embrace. We get hugged when we experience God.

In Acts 10:44, Peter is preaching to a group of Gentiles who were considered outcasts. They had been referred to as dogs. Even Peter had difficulty going to minister to them and only did so after God supernaturally spoke to him in a dream. These were outcasts, much like us. But as Peter is preaching to them about Jesus Christ, the Bible says the Holy Spirit "fell upon all who were listening to the message." The Greek word used in this verse for "fell on them" is the same word used in our story for the Father "falling on the lost son and embracing him."

How interesting! When you received Christ, you received the Holy Spirit into your heart. You got hugged by a loving, warm, compassionate Father who had sought you out.

No matter what view you have had of God in the past, today you will start seeing God in a new light. You will see him for who He is, a Father who receives you as a full-fledged child! No matter what you have done, your heavenly Father accepts you back into the household as an heir.

"For you did not receive a spirit that makes you a slave again to fear, but you received the Spirit of sonship. And by him we cry, 'Abba,'

Father. The Spirit himself testifies with our
spirit that we are God's children. Now if we are
children, then we are heirs — heirs of God and
co-heirs with Christ, if indeed we share in his
sufferings in order that we may also share in his
glory." (Romans 8:15-17)

Whoever does not love does not know
God, because God is love. This is how God showed
his love among us: He sent his one and only Son
into the world that we might live through him.
This is love: not that we loved God, but that he
loved us and sent his Son as an atoning sacrifice
for our sins. (I John 4:8-10)

Thought to Ponder

Do I have a healthy view of God?

Do I see God as a loving Father?

step five
stay humble

realize who you are not (without God)

"I have sinned against heaven and against you. I am no longer worthy to be called your son..." (Luke 15:21)

eight
steps to a
brand new
life

We have been accepted back into the family by our Father. Now what? Well, today's step is stay humble. The first response of the prodigal was, "I am no longer worthy to be called your son." (Luke 15:21)

The new reality is just the opposite. He was a son and not a slave. So are we.

"Because you are sons, God sent the Spirit of his Son into our hearts, the Spirit who calls out, 'Abba, Father.' So you are no longer a slave, but a son; and since you are a son, God has made you also an heir." (Galatians 4:6-7)

Yet our response must be the same as that of the prodigal - "I am no longer worthy." In other words, I do not deserve being accepted into heaven. I do not deserve being restored as a child of God. It's because of amazing grace and not anything I've done.

Always realize who you would be without God's amazing grace.

This must be our ongoing attitude. You see, sin thrives on arrogant self-sufficiency. This is called the pride of life and we must resist pride at all costs. This is what got us into trouble in the beginning. Pride is doing life our way, not God's way.

We must daily humble ourselves under the mighty hand of God and trust God to promote us.

The best way we can do this is by trusting in the Word of God. The Bible is the Word of God and it is our guide for living. We must commit to obeying God every day by receiving His Word and doing what it says.

Obedience is the best way to stay humble before God. Commit to a daily time of reading the Bible and meditating on it. Your coach can help you learn to study the Bible for yourself. Your pastor can help explain the meaning of the Bible so that you can practically apply it to your everyday life.

Stay humble by reading the Bible every day.

Stay humble by listening to your pastor every week.

Stay humble by talking to your coach about how to apply the Bible to your life.

Stay humble by listening to the voice of the Holy Spirit. Let the Spirit who lives in you speak to you through your conscience.

You will never go wrong by staying humble before God.

"But He gives us more grace. That is why

Scripture says: 'God opposes the proud but gives grace to the humble.' Submit yourselves, then, to God. Resist the devil, and he will flee from you." (James 4:6-7)

Scripture says: God opposes the proud but gives grace to the humble.' Submit yourselves, then to God. Resist the devil, and he will flee from you.' (James 4:6-7).

Thought to Ponder

How have I already heard the voice of God this week?

Have I quickly obeyed?

step six
dress up

*realize who you are
(with God)*
"Bring the best robe and put it on
him." (Luke 15:22)

eight
steps to a
brand new
life

Today's step is to dress up.

When the prodigal returned home and began to say how he was not worthy to be a son, the Father interrupted him (the sentence in Luke 15:21 is not completed in the original manuscripts) and more than reversed the direction the son was heading. Instead of allowing the son to be just a "hired man" in the house, the Father outfits him with a robe, a ring, and a pair of shoes.

The robe was a ceremonial one that a guest of honor would receive. The ring signified authority. The sandals were those only a free man would wear. This was no wardrobe for a slave.

The robe in the Bible also represents righteousness. Our dress reflects our identity. This step of dressing up is all about realizing who we are in God! We are made the righteousness of God because of the death and resurrection of Jesus Christ. When you received God, you put on Christ. You became God's righteousness.

On the cross, your sins were logged onto Jesus' account and Jesus' righteousness was credited to your account. This is the great exchange. The Bible uses an accounting term to describe this exchange. Our sins are debited out of our account into Jesus' account. And in turn, God's righteousness is credited to our account from the account of Jesus Christ.

The term is "imputation." Christianity is more about imputation than imitation. Our sins are attributed to Christ on the cross and his righteousness is attributed to us. An exchange has taken place on heaven's accounting rolls.

Wow! We are not under the burden to imitate a perfect Jesus in order to have a right standing before God. All religions offer steps to imitating God. And all religions fail. We cannot in ourselves imitate God. This is religious folly.

Only Christianity offers imputation. Christ took our place on the cross. Jesus became the once-and- for-all vicar, our High Priest. He acted on our behalf and died a vicarious death. He took our place.

This is what has happened to you regardless of how you feel or don't feel. Each day now you must by faith realize who you are with God. You are righteous and justified before God.

Thought to Ponder

> Why do I find it hard to realize that
> I am forgiven and stand righteous
> before God?

step seven
eat up

look to God for fulfillment
"Bring the fattened calf and kill it.
Let's have a feast."
(Luke 15:23)

eight
steps to a
brand new
life

Our story continues with the Father throwing a party. He kills the fattened calf and invites everyone to a feast. Our seventh step is to eat up!

This means to look to God for fulfillment and meaning, not just in the beginning but for all your days.

"Blessed are the poor in spirit, for theirs is the kingdom of heaven. Blessed are those who mourn, for they will be comforted. Blessed are the meek, for they will inherit the earth. Blessed are those who hunger and thirst for righteousness, for they will be filled." (Matthew 5:3-6)

God delights in filling the appetites of those who hunger after him. Too often we look for fulfillment in all the wrong places. This gets us into trouble. You must see your Christian faith as a daily lifestyle, not just a "Sunday extra." You must look to your relationship with God, not your past "watering holes," to find fulfillment. In other words, we must change our eating places and drinking spots.

The tendency is to simply add religion as one more thing. But we must resist this notion and radically make our relationship with

God the replacement to those other sources of fulfillment.

Our lifestyle changes, not just because we are avoiding the old negative influences, but because we are adding the positive influences associated with our new life. God is replacing the old with the new.

Your Christianity must be more about what you add to your life than what you take away. Your steps to change must be positive reinforcements, not negative rules. Your hangouts, hobbies and habits change because the new ones bring fulfillment, whereas the old ones brought emptiness.

Christianity is more about feasting than fasting. It's more about your relationship and not your religion. It's more about what you can do than what you can't do.

You are feeding the new life that will grow and you are replacing the old life that was going nowhere.

Thought to Ponder

What are some things I can do daily
to help establish my new Christian
lifestyle?

step eight
party hard

live life to the full
"So they began to celebrate."
(Luke 15:24)

eight
steps to a
brand new
life

The party is underway and it's being thrown by the Father. Why? His son was dead and is now alive again. His son was lost and is now found. When we are saved, a party scene breaks out in heaven. There is music and dancing. There is food and lots of it.

Our eighth step is to party hard.

Live life to the full.

We have a reason to rejoice. We were dead. Think about the powerful emotion of grief that manifests in death. Death produces the strong emotion of grief. But think about life replacing death. Resurrection produces the strong emotion of joy. We are commanded in the Bible to rejoice!

"Rejoice in the Lord always. I will say it again: Rejoice!" (Philippians 4:4)

Christianity's signature emotion is joy. We are a happy religion. Yet so many churches are anything but emotionally jubilant. Church should be a celebration. We come together primarily to rejoice. And we do this in a worship setting that includes music and dancing. If we want to emulate the party scene of our story, we must have a celebration that invites us to rejoice with music and dancing. Such should be the Sunday norm. Such is the pattern of heaven.

"The Lord your God is with you, he is mighty to save. He will take great delight in you, he will quiet you with his love, he will rejoice over you with singing.The sorrows for the appointed feasts I will remove from you; they are a burden and a reproach to you. At that time I will deal with all who oppressed you; I will rescue the lame and gather those who have been scattered. I will give them praise and honor in every land where they were put to shame. At that time I will gather you; at that time I will bring you home. I will give you honor and praise among all the peoples of the earth when I restore your fortunes before your very eyes," says the Lord." (Zephaniah 3:17-19)

The word "rejoice" means to display joy. Heaven displays joy - dances if you will. As we come together to celebrate, we too should display joy. Our celebrating should be indicative of heaven's.

As we celebrate on Sunday, we begin to set teh tone for what will happen all week. We live life to the full every day, not just Sunday.

Sunday is the model for this new life and an important part of this eighth step. In the Bible, the number eight represents new beginnings. Sunday is the eighth day, the day of new beginnings. It is the day of resurrection, the first day to something new and not the last day to something old. We come week after week, not out of religious habit, but out of a desire for a fresh, new start to our week.

We begin the eight steps all over again.

We wake up.

We get up.

We go home.

We get hugged.

We stay humble.

We dress up.

We eat up.

We party hard.

These are eight steps to a brand new life!

Thought to Ponder

How can I make sure my faith stays
fresh and vibrant?

How can I avoid the trappings of the
religious mind?

now what?
commit to the church

Where do you go from here? It's simple. You're on a journey. You've taken those first "baby steps," but you must keep on keeping on.

Here are some important suggestions:

1. Attend church every Sunday. Make sure you're in a church that celebrates every Sunday. Enthusiastic worship is the signature of a redeemed community.

Make sure the church believes the Bible. It contains the answers for your life.

Make sure the church preaches that Jesus is the only answer for our sinful state and that the cross is center to everything.

Make sure the church believes in the work of the Holy Spirit today.

Create the habit of starting your week off meeting with other believers in an atmosphere that closely resembles the celebrative atmosphere of heaven. Your Christian faith was never meant to be lived "solo," but in community with others who have also been brought back from the dead.

If you received Christ in a church that introduced you to this book, that is probably the church for you.

2. Commit to a class. These eight days

are a great starter to your new life, but the journey continues. Get in a class that explains what has happened to you from a Biblical perspective.

Begin to pursue truth and seek to understand the profound yet simple teachings of the Bible.

3. Get baptized. One of our first acts of obedience is to be baptized. Talk to your coach or pastor about this important step to sealing your faith in Christ.

4. Join a small group. The church is more than Sunday. Find a small group that you can plug into within the church. Look to this group for connection, care and a continuing growth path in the faith. Make sure the group offers the integrity of authentic relationships and accountability. Begin to connect to others and find ways to join with them in serving others. The sooner you become a contributor to God's work, the better.

5. Spend daily time with God. You have come into a personal relationship with God. Christianity is a faith and not a religion. Relationships must be cultivated. We do this from the first day of our new life until the day we die and go to heaven by reading our Bibles and praying. Set aside time each day to read certain passages (entire books like the Gospel of John or chapters like Romans 8). Treat prayer like a two-way communication. Talk to God AND listen for God to speak to you. Journal your thoughts. Talk to your coach about how to listen for the voice of God in your life. You can do this without becoming weird or other-worldly.

6. Share your story. Start sharing with others now. Tell your story. Let people know what God is doing in your life. Don't be afraid to "witness" to others. Again, as you start sharing, consult with your coach.

7. Keep taking the eight steps. These steps don't stop today. These eight steps are vital to your ongoing new life and are good habits to create.

Realize your ongoing need for God.

Make a decision every day to keep changing.

Stay on track and get back up when you "fall off the wagon."

Continue to see God in a new light as your loving heavenly Father.

Keep realizing who you aren't without God.

And keep realizing who you are in God.

Look to God every day for fulfillment and meaning.

And don't forget to live life to the full every day.

You were made for more. Don't settle for less.

Congratulations on the new life!

"Therefore, if anyone is in Christ,
he is a new creation;
the old has gone,
the new has come!"

2 Corinthians 5:17